CHILDREN
OF
EVE

Kevin Casey

DEDICATED

to

Ace, Amber, Bay-Girl, Bones, Lobo, Axe, Gypsy, Morbid, Marsh, Kini, Peaches, Lucky, Quebec, Dr. Death, Cat, Kitten, Space, Little Space, Wisdom, Wish, Worm, Wrath, Zebra, Dragon, Turtle, Outback, Sin, Priest, Satan, Angel, Beaker, Mignon, Reed, Bug, Shorty, Too Tall, Prince, Snake, Crappy, Samurai, Poop-stain, Baby Boy, Confused, Starchild, Red, Sasha, Fanny, Alexia, Nina, Marilyn, Sequoia, Jesse, Connie, Stacy, Brittany, Rock-Ann, Cayote, Breeze, Tweaky Dave, Punisher, Punisher II, Baser, Miown, Cupcake, Sad, Patience, Insane, Shakespeare, Soda-pop, Whisper, Chance, Rag Doll, Quiet, Happy, Smiley, Bambi, Candy, Stormy, Stare, Sprite, Sweet-T, Chief, Mischief, Houston, Trash, Mystic, Undertaker, Ratt, D-day, Riff-raff, Ricochet, Robin, Hood, Puck, Catfish, Dopey, Cherry, Kong, Animal, Tranc, Pockets, Bunny, Frostbite, Dusty, Borg, Weedhopper, Nikki, Gadget, Skyy, Christmas, Hutch, Shadow, Crystle, Precious, Silver, Gem, Sapphire, Tiara, Wolf, Wolfette, Little John, Little One, Little Bit, Cat Eyes, Joy, Sunny, Tex, Daisy, Miss T-Bird, Skywalker, Starmonkey, Polo, Giggles, Happenin', Ice, Loaded, Misty, Craft, Raven, Baron, Coda, Hawk, Shaggy, Shytown, Honey, Moondrop, Brandy, Raccoon, Lizard, Gidget, Butterfly, Skunk, and the many other kids who, to hide something, to be something, or wanting to believe it was cool to be homeless, re-named themselves.

Table Of Contents

Introduction

by Sister Mary Rose McGeady

You've opened a book that tells the story of a modern American tragedy. The story about America's homeless kids.

The kids you'll meet in this book come from everywhere and nowhere, the suburbs and the slums, in all shapes and sizes. But as different as they are, they all have one thing in common — each one of these kids you'll meet has no sense of belonging to anyone, any place anything. They are *disconnected*.

We discover them broke, tired, homeless, and most of all, lonely. They come to our Covenant House crisis shelters because, quite simply, they have no place else to go.

In talking with these kids about what has brought them to us, we hear many things again and again.

Many have long histories of sexual abuse, or physical or emotional neglect.

Some come from families burdened with drug or alcohol addiction, or psychological and emotional problems.

Many are stepchildren, casualties of the growing incidence of divorce and remarriage.

Or they are kids who don't have families at all: raised in foster homes or in institutions, then aging out of the system by eighteen, or simply walking away at an earlier age without looking back.

Other young men are fleeing the destruction that war has brought to their homes and families in Central America. They leave behind towns stricken with poverty, come north to Los Angeles pursuing a dream akin to the one that founded our country.

These are all objectively bad situations, and while running away is not the best response in many cases, it is often a sign that this child is healthy in a place wrought with sickness. Many of these kids were the only ones in their environment brave enough to say, "There is something wrong here, and I won't live this way." Then they find themselves on the street.

This book charts the fallout from our shifting culture as seen through the eyes of our counselors on the front lines of this struggle. These are caring adults who try day and night to reach these kids, to re-connect them to society, to healthy lives, to the love of God.

The founder of my religious order, St. Vincent de Paul, taught us that before we can teach the poor about God we must first take care of their bodily needs. At Covenant House, we can't tell a kid God loves her if she's dirty, cold, hungry, and sick.

Words like love don't work on our kids. We are challenged as Christians to *show* our kids we love them, not tell them.

So this is also a book about a machine, a concrete, material presence in the lives of the kids we try to save. It's a blue 1988 custom Chevy van (with a white dove on the side, the symbol of Covenant House) that goes out into the streets every night searching for homeless kids.

Our van counselors are on the street most of the night, from seven in the evening to four or five in the morning. They meet teen prostitutes, homeless youth, and hard-core street kids. What they face is often unpredictable. In a span of minutes, they are called upon to do everything from handing a hungry child a sandwich to taking a razor blade from a youth with freshly slashed wrists.

Whether a child needs medical attention, food, clothing, or shelter, it can be arranged immediately. If the child needs to talk, to cry, to sort things out, the van team is there as well.

On a night that's bitter cold or wet, there may be as many as ten kids huddled in the van, soaking in the warmth of the heater, eating sandwiches, and sipping hot chocolate.

An hour later there may be one child in the warm van, exhausted and alone, who called from the bus station or a payphone and heard, "OK, we're in the van. We know where you are. We're turning onto the freeway now. I want you to stay on the line until you actually see us pull up in front of you and wave. OK?"

With this same phone, the van team can work with hospitals, police stations, shelters, parents and relatives, whatever the child needs . . . wherever the child is. Many of the kids wouldn't step foot in an office with its desks and intimidating forms and counselors, so we bring a different kind of office to them.

And so of course, this is a book about a very special group of people, a group I am proud of, our street outreach team.

Please, I ask you to take the time to read this book, to learn about these brave people, our kids and our staff (it won't take long!) And if you can spare a few minutes more, please pray for courage and strength for our staff that we may be effective instruments of God's love and for human dignity for our troubled youth. And pray, please, that healthy, loving famly life may become a priority in our parishes, in our schools, and most importantly, in our own homes.

> In God's love,
> Sr. Mary Rose McGeady
> New York, August, 1991

Chapter 1

Lisa is a spent shell. She lies gleaming on the sidewalk in the hot California sun.

"Hi, Lisa," I call, passing in the van, en route from Covenant House to Venice to find two tired kids who called seeking shelter.

"Hey," she salutes hoarsely. Lisa is a Hollywood street kid, perhaps the one I love the most, though she'll never know it.

The curb, and the city of Los Angeles, is a dry and dusty place in the summer, which lasts about eight months. Then we have fall for a little while, and then it's summer again.

"You've got to remember," Lisa often says, "this is a desert. Somebody came along and there was absolutely nothing and he said, let's build a city *here*. Now there are millions of people living here, stuck here. We're running out of water.

"It's a desert," she says, shaking her head, waving an arm at the dark green ivy sloping up from the freeway. "If you don't water it, it'll wither; it'll die."

She speaks as much of herself as the land.

Lisa was born and has lived her entire life within walking distance of Hollywood Boulevard and Bronson Avenue, a block from where Hollywood Boulevard crosses the Hollywood Freeway, five blocks from Covenant House.

She stands, brushing the sidewalk grit from the seat of her jeans. What Lisa wears is an American adolescent uniform: jeans and white sneakers, a t-shirt, and a button down cotton shirt. The latter is too large and hangs loosely from the thin frame.

Standing on the corner of Hollywood and Bronson, tall and pale, long weathered locks of auburn hair swinging around her shoulders, her arms hanging at her side, Lisa looks like an urban scarecrow. Like most rural scarecrows, there's nothing particularly frightening about her, to birds, to anybody. She's just a kid, eighteen, and she lives on the street.

What to do today, she thinks, having stood up for some reason. Her stomach provides the answer as it does every morning, with an acidic twinge and its own gastric dialogue. Today she will eat.

Like most of the people in the third world and in Los Angeles, Lisa is beginning a day in which her considerable efforts will ultimately put food in her stomach.

What direction those efforts take is very much up to her.

She sets off towards the touristy strip of Hollywood Boulevard, where for a dozen blocks the concrete turns black and stars appear, imbedded in the sidewalk and labeled with the names of a lot of people nobody remembers.

Lisa grew up here, but she's seen so many runaways drawn to Hollywood from somewhere else by the promise of paradise offered in the movies.

For what, she wonders: for pimps and drug dealers, pizza places and tattoo parlors, and for homeless kids like herself, asking for change.

"How can you do that?" a friend on the street asks. "I can't panhandle. I get embarrassed."

"If you're embarrassed you're not hungry enough," Lisa says. She's only embarrassed when cute boys her age pass by. Then she pretends she's combing her hair in the store window.

"Forget this change stuff," her friend says, "Come make money with me."

Lisa once again has the opportunity to sell cocaine for tremendous amounts of money. Being a dealer is near the top of the street survival food chain. She'd have a lot of money to play with and she could make out well if she kept her head about her. It's pretty dangerous, though.

Moving down the chain, she could steal cars or just car radios, break into houses, or rob people of their wallets and leather jackets on the streets at night.

Lisa knows the score: someone has to suffer if you want to survive on the street in Hollywood. It's either somebody else, or it's you. If you decide to take the suffering on yourself, you can sell your body, panhandle, or eat out of dumpsters. After three years on the street, Lisa chooses to panhandle.

"No thanks, man," Lisa tells her coke dealer friend hoarsely, looking down. "I'm fine."

This way nobody else gets hurt.

Lisa's been hurt enough by people here: other kids, not so benign drug dealers, and her parents. She knows how it feels. Her mother overdosed on prescribed antidepressants. Her dad became distant, unable to cope with the pain of his wife's suicide and the stress of raising his only daughter.

Strong of character and independent, Lisa had done her best to stay out of the way. And she'd been working hard. But her grades dropped one semester and nothing was said. Then she came home drunk at four one morning and no one noticed. Soon there were nights she didn't come home. Her dad never mentioned it.

After a prolonged absence of three nights— nights of walking, reading, sleeping on the beach—she was sure her dad would have something to say to her. Anything. Lisa came home to find the house locks changed and her t-shirts, jeans, and cassette tapes on the back steps. This intelligent, thoughtful girl withered. Two and a half years ago, at sixteen, Lisa became a Hollywood street kid.

Somewhere in this desert, there had to be someone with love to spare for Lisa.

HOW TO DEFUSE
AN ANGRY TEENAGER

No one likes to deal with an angry person, but a certain amount of teenage anger is inevitable. Often, the key to success is to understand your child better by finding out where the anger is coming from, and then adjusting your own behavior to help your teenager overcome the underlying problems that are causing the anger.

If your child is given to angry outbursts, here are some suggestions that should help you negotiate a truce.

Don't panic. Even if you feel that you don't recognize your own child anymore accept it for the moment.

Listen carefully to what your teenager is blurting out to you. Try to read between the lines to find out what the real issue is. Although your teen's insults, complaints and demands may be hurting you, they are actually cries for help.

Don't retaliate. Don't come up with threats and punishments without trying to find out why your teen is angry. Parental retaliation against teenage anger often makes the situation worse.

Tell him that he's hurting you—not in such a way as to make him feel guilty—but in a way that will make him realize that you're concerned and just trying to understand what's bothering him.

Reexamine the rules. At a non-angry time try to explain to your teen that although there absolutely have to be rules in the house, perhaps some of the "old rules" can be adjusted. Negotiate to develop rules you can both live with.

Chapter 2

Two years ago at a family picnic, Tim watched his father put a bullet into his mother's head. His father momentarily trained the gun on Tim, but dropped it and waited silently for the police to come. His father went to prison. Tim went to a group home. He was thirteen.

At fourteen he was placed with a foster family, who were nice, stable people and told him he could stay as long as he wanted. "You can grow up here," they said. "Be part of our family."

"You are not my parents," he responded, refusing their love. It clashed violently with a deep feeling that he was worthless, and triggered an inner turmoil that sent him running to Hollywood. Now he lay under a thin gray blanket on the steps of Sunset Boulevard's Blessed Sacrament Church, hungry and cold at night.

This suffering reinforced his belief that he was bad, and actually stabilized his world. But choosing to sleep at the door of a church expressed his unutterable need for redemption. Nevertheless, he consistently rejected the help of the Jesuit Fathers of Blessed Sacrament.

"I'm Tim," the boy said to us, rising.

We met Tim while bustling in for Mass. It was the day after we arrived to open Covenant House Los Angeles in November of 1988. Six of us stood around on the church steps, a rather frightful greeting for him, I imagine. He was about five foot four inches tall, with straight black hair and mocha-colored skin, but painfully thin. We introduced ourselves awkwardly.

"I . . . I really don't want to go to a shelter," Tim stuttered when we told him about our work. But he let Robert get him a hamburger at the grease-pit across the street. When Robert returned we lingered a little too long and Tim became nervous and edgy.

"I've uh, got to meet somebody now," Tim said, gathering up his blanket and his little transistor radio with a broken antenna.

We left him alone, and he sat back down.

"Can't the police do something," I asked Micheline as we walked down Sunset Boulevard after Mass. "He's just a kid!"

"He's not a *criminal,*" she said, "and he'd probably just run from any shelter they put him in. Then he'd be back where he started. Only he wouldn't trust us. He's got to decide to come in himself if anything is going to work for him."

Micheline had worked outreach in New York before coming to Los Angeles. I saw the sense of what she was saying.

By calling the police, I would be meeting *my need* to see Tim off the street immediately, but it would just reinforce his belief that he was bad. He'd sink deeper into his despair, and feel betrayed by us as well.

"Give him time, be good to him, he'll come around," Micheline said. "It's the only way. Believe me, Kevin."

When I first decided to volunteer at Covenant House, I figured all I'd have to do was tell kids there was a place to go and they'd rush gratefully in.

But somewhere along the line Tim had been convinced, probably by someone whose love he needed very much, that he was worthless. I was only now beginning to see how feelings of unworthiness and mistrust keep innocent kids like Tim from accepting the help they need and deserve.

So we sat on the steps talking with Tim for a few minutes every day, always with something to eat and a soda or a milk.

Some days, Tim showed me stories he jotted in a blue spiral notebook as he sat all night on the church steps. In every story a child was being hatcheted or beheaded or shot or disemboweled. This boy needs help, I thought. How much longer can we wait?

A week later it was chilly and drizzling. I pulled on a sweater before we set off for Blessed Sacrament Church. When we got there, Tim lay under his dirty blanket, fully clothed and in a fetal position for warmth.

But Tim wasn't just cold, he was sick: shaking uncontrollably, grimacing, and breathing in quick, shallow pants. Four hours ago he'd run to his blanket racked with chills. Now a feverish sweat ran from his forehead soaking his hair.

He stood shakily, looking as if he'd been caught in a downpour. His jeans and his green plaid shirt were drenched with perspiration.

"C-C-Can I come back with you guys?" he stammered.

We put Tim on a cot in our warm office with a few clean, thick blankets. Dave and I sat in the next room all night, playing cards. For the first hour Tim's staccato cough bounced loudly into our room. Then Tim slept, his breath calling and answering in rough phrases all night.

Micheline would be in at nine a.m. to take him to the free clinic. In addition to being a great prayer leader at the Faith Community house, she was a social worker and could network with other social workers. Somewhere between the church steps and the system, with equal parts of compassion and therapy, Tim would find his redemption.

HOW TO TALK TO YOUR TEEN

Listen, really listen. Don't try to listen while doing something else. Put your chores aside so your teen knows you're really paying attention.

Tolerate differences. View your teenager as an individual distinct from you. But this doesn't mean you can't state your opinion if you disagree.

Never imply that your teenager's feelings don't matter or that they will change. Teens live in the present. It doesn't help them to know they'll soon feel differently.

Chapter 3

Lisa walked more briskly than usual through the streets of Hollywood, mostly to conceal the fact that today she had nowhere to go. She strode into every record shop on Hollywood Boulevard, diligently checking through their bins of albums for a certain record which, it always appeared, she couldn't find.

"Can I help you with something?" the proprietor asked.

"I'm looking for Umagumma, the Pink Floyd album," she said, knowing it wasn't in the rack.

After a brief search, he offered, "Oh, well, we can order it for you . . ."

"No. That's fine," Lisa declined, heading back to the sidewalk. "I need it today."

She didn't have a dime in her pocket. Freshly exiled from her father's house, she needed something to do. A mission. Something to busy herself, to hold off the panic that threatened to overwhelm her if she stopped, if she slowed down, if she started to think.

After exhausting the record shops she rummaged through the movie-still and poster stores in search of an obscure color photo of the musician Roger Waters. "Yeah, he's hammering on a gong on top of an empty stadium in Pompeii. I've seen it before," Lisa explained. This item also proved impossible to find.

"Do these people know," she thought, walking quickly past Hollywood High, "that I don't have anywhere to go? Can they tell, as I walk by, that I am not a student here, that I am hungry, that I have nowhere to sleep tonight?"

For an hour or so she pretended to be waiting for someone at Tomy's Burgers on Hollywood Boulevard. It's a narrow place, dimly lit, with a simple counter and a grill. There's enough room for ten small tables between one white wall and the row of windows that look out on an unremarkable Wilcox Avenue.

Then the pride and the energy that would have had her moving on to another place deserted Lisa. She just sat, staring at the floor as day turned to night. A fast acculturation began as she watched street kids come and go from the all-night hang out. An icy panic inched up her legs and frosted her sides as she slowly realized she was now one of them.

In the chiseled young faces around her, she saw a hard-core, cool stance that seemed to say, "I can survive against this screwed up, evil world." She was drawn to it. She wanted to believe she, too, could walk these streets every day without terror or confusion. What she wouldn't know until later, until it was too late, is that underneath their cool masks they were feeling exactly what she felt now.

"Hey, Jammer," one long-haired boy shouted, greeting another with a handshake that resembled a mid-air arm wrestle. They all had street names: Shakespeare, Bandit, Skunk, Angel, Smiley, Toy, Punk.

She liked the anonymity, the freedom from the past, the control over the future, over one's destiny, that was suggested by the act of renaming yourself.

An attractive young man in a tie-dyed Grateful Dead shirt walked up to her, knotting his long blonde hair into a pony-tail. "Where you from?" he asked. "You're new. I'm Bitter."

"Colorado," Lisa answered in her slow, throaty voice. "I'm Stray."

The lie. The name. They afforded her only a modicum of protection and power. But it was enough. Like Hollywood itself, the image alone went a long way in influencing the people around her and bolstering her fears.

Before long, she would be hard-core herself. The cool mask would serve her so well she would rarely feel safe enough to take it off. And the longer it stayed on, the more fights she skirted, the more dumpsters she scavenged, the more of her values she overlooked to survive, the tighter the mask would become.

Soon the very parts of Stray the mask was designed to protect, the parts of her that fell in love, that trusted, that she had put away for safekeeping, would no longer be available even to Stray herself. She would become thickly mired in her own misery, loneliness and desperation—all beneath a cool, unconcerned mask.

But that first night, as dawn turned an unusually overcast sky gunmetal grey, it was exhaustion that temporarily pushed away Stray's panic, dissolved her worry of what to do next. She settled between two bushes at Barnsdall

Art Park farther east down Hollywood Boulevard. This is a quiet park, I should be fine, she began to think. But too tired to care any more, she abandoned her tight control over the situation and fell asleep. When she woke it was dark again, and her stomach was clenching in mutiny.

WHAT TO DO IF YOU THINK YOUR TEEN IS USING DRUGS

First, you must understand the four levels of drug use: experimentation, controlled use, abuse, and dependence—and then react accordingly.

Experimentation. If your child is just starting to try drugs, the worst thing you could do is accuse him of being a "drug fiend." Overreaction can actually make the child use drugs more—in rebellion.

Instead, be subtle. Quietly tell him you feel he may be getting into something dangerous. Don't accuse or lecture. Ask why he wants to try drugs, and explain that you don't want drugs to interfere with his health and his goals in life.

Controlled use refers to the occasional drug user. In this case, the person does not allow the drug to control him, or interfere with his work. Again, in this situation, it is best to approach your child gently with your concerns, without overreacting.

Abuse. People cross the line from controlled use to abuse when they start using drugs frequently and excessively. If you're convinced your child is an abuser, tell him you love him and want to help him with his problem. If he doesn't stop, convince him to go to a counselor with you.

Dependence occurs when the drug controls the person. In this case, the user is self-destructive and you must act decisively and forcefully. Carry your child to a treatment center if you have to.

Chapter 4

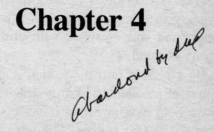

"Paging Ronald Marsh. Ronald Marsh, please report to the information booth."

A police officer at the bus station had helped Micheline and John search for the four stranded boys; but they couldn't be found. "Hold on a minute," the officer then said, slipping into an office behind the ticket booth. Now his voice was echoing over the station intercom.

A chain of four little boys, holding hands, appeared at the information booth a minute later.

The officer smiled. Ronald, the oldest boy at sixteen, was leading them. He had called our crisis line. Behind him, his brothers marched in size order. Hughie was fifteen, Leonard thirteen, and Robbie just twelve. They'd been tucked away in a corner of the inner waiting room.

The bus terminal in Downtown L. A. is large, grey, has escalators that work sometimes, and was designed with utility and not beauty in mind.

Just getting into the station is an obstacle course of transients and drug dealers. They offer to help overburdened travellers with their bags at the taxi station. The wise don't hand over a thing. Those who've been here before politely decline and swiftly go upstairs. They purchase their tickets, flash them to the guard, and pass to relative safety within the walls of the ticketed passenger waiting area.

The seats are hard, green plastic and the rows of fluorescent lights will fatigue you. But you can get a paper and a cup of coffee up there and well, sit and wait for your bus.

The four boys weren't ticketed, but Ronald could tell it was the safest part of the bus station. He'd managed to put himself and his brothers where he knew the junkies and pushers downstairs couldn't go. He was nervous, shaking. He told Micheline their story haltingly, overloaded with anxiety and the weight of responsibility for his little brothers.

The boys and their mother left Chicago a week earlier to visit their dad in California. Their parents had been separated only a month. Perhaps this was their mother's attempt at reconciliation, or a way to remind her husband that he still had children to care for. She could only get a week off from work and had to return early, but the kids were to stay another two weeks. This morning their dad took the boys to the station to see their mom off.

They waved good-bye to their mom. The bus pulled away. They turned to leave and their father was gone. He'd ditched them. He sped off in his car with the money for the boys' tickets home. The money their mom had given him.

What kind of monster could abandon four little kids like these, Micheline wondered, and in a nasty place like this? What did he think would happen to them? Where did he think they would go? What did he think they would do?

Behind the boys on the bus terminal floor, where their dad had been standing, was a black plastic garbage sack. Inside it they discovered their clothes, some cheezy California souvenirs they'd bought in Hollywood, and a large

white polar bear that Leonard, the second
youngest, had won at Knott's Berry Farm.

"I asked my dad why he was carrying that
bag when we got out of the car," Ronald said,
confused. "He said he was dumping the trash
at the bus station. But it was *our stuff!*" Merci-
fully, the child even now didn't grasp what his
father had meant by trash.

Knowing he could never find his dad's
apartment again in the jumble of freeways and
streets they'd travelled, Ronald insisted they
all stay inside and stick together. He chose not
to speak to the police officer or the security
guard. He called the operator, who put him
through to the Covenant House Nineline.

The Nineline is our twenty-four hour toll
free crisis line for runaways, troubled kids and
their parents. A million kids call us a year. In
Los Angeles, two or three kids call every week
from this very bus station, as Ronald had. I
guess he felt a lot safer talking on the phone,
where he could feel us out from a distance.

Hughie, fifteen, was sad and ashamed and
wouldn't speak to Micheline or John. The two
younger boys, unaware of their situation
played happily with the armrest of the escala-

tor, pretending it was their strength that sent it
down to the first floor.

Their mother was en route to Chicago, but
Micheline located their grandmother's number
through Chicago phone information. "Lord
save us," the woman cried on the phone. "Are
they all right? Can I speak to Ronnie?"

Ronald took the phone without emotion.
"Yes, Gramma . . . . Yes . . . . No . . . . *He just
left.* No, *these people* are here." He held the
phone out to Micheline. "She wants to know
what's gonna happen."

The boy's grandmother was very poor and
couldn't afford one child's ticket, much less
four. The police officer, still standing quietly
nearby, caught the gist of the conversation.
"Tell her no problem," he whispered to
Micheline.

The officer stepped to the front of the ticket
line and returned with four blank ticket vouch-
ers. "Greyhound will pay for their tickets. It's
called the Home Free Program. I just have to
write a report saying they're runaways. A tech-
nicality." He jotted their names and ages on a
pad. "The tickets will be waiting for them in
the morning. The next bus to Chicago leaves
bright and early at seven."

John told me later that from where he was standing ten feet away he could hear the grandmother's tinny phone voice shouting something about Jesus. "Bless you. Bless you," she told Micheline.

The kids slept on the cot and couches at our office. Micheline woke me at 4:30 a.m. to buy food for their trip and to get them back to the station by 7:00 a.m.

"You're a brave guy," I told Ron as he ushered the yawning little guys onto their bus to Chicago. "Your brothers are lucky to have you."

He didn't answer me.

When old bro becomes dad; is now mature than his father —

HOW TO BE YOUR TEEN'S BEST FRIEND

Set aside some quality time to share with your teen on a regular basis.

Find some activity you can enjoy together. It can be as simple as taking a walk, going to a show or the movies, or perhaps just going to a restaurant together.

Be honest with your teen. When you're angry or disappointed, explain why. When you're happy, share your joy. Give praise and encouragement when you're pleased with your teen's behavior or accomplishments.

Be a good listener.

Trust your teen to "do the right thing" after you've offered your advice and guidance.

Forgive and forget. Everybody makes mistakes. Allow your teen to learn from them.

Say "I love you."

Chapter 5

"Are you, *like,* affiliated with *Christ* in any way?" she slashed.

After two weeks of living on the street in Hollywood, Lisa, aka "Stray," crossed paths with our Covenant House van for the first time.

I remember thinking she was probably sixteen—under all that white powder and death-black lipstick, maybe younger. She wore black: shoes, tights, a short leather skirt, a tube top, and a leather jacket. Her hair, what was left of it after the sides of her head were shaved clean, was also jet black, though dyed, and sort of pony-tailed by a bright pink clip. The Harley Barbie ensemble, I thought. This one's got to be a street kid. No girl's mother would let her look like this.

I hadn't even spoken and she couldn't stand me. She'd been skipping casually through the tourists crowding Hollywood Boulevard on a Friday night when the van pulled alongside her. She glared disdainfully at the Covenant House card I extended hopefully in one hand, at the white dove on the van, the dove on my baby blue jacket and then at me.

"Are you, *like*, affiliated with *Christ* in any way?" she'd demanded. She was waiting for an answer.

Why didn't they tell me it was going to be this hard? What could I say? God, help me, I prayed. So many things ran through my head in that instant.

Should I say yes? I knew she'd just moan and write me off as another irrelevant tract-pushing street-corner evangelist. If I let this happen she might never talk to someone from Covenant House again, and we won't be able to help her.

But if I say no, I'll be denying the very root of my being, and my motive for doing this. My head ached with it.

Covenant House is run by a nun, Sister Mary Rose. But no kid has to pray before he or she can eat one of our sandwiches. Not one

bible study is required before or after we send
a street kid to the doctor, or to a drug program.
A kid can get a bus home, or ride the van to
shelter, and not even believe in God.

If we made kids pray most wouldn't let us
help them. And helping them is our job.

In truth, it *is* all about God—every sandwich, every runaway sent home, every homeless kid asleep on a clean bed in our house. But
there's a certain subtlety to the way we are
called to work in the kids' presence. It probably comes from the humbling knowledge that
their angels in heaven always see the face of
our Father in heaven.

As a member of the volunteer faith community, I had made a year-long commitment not
just to serve the kids of Covenant House, but
also to live simply, chastely, and to pray with
my fellow community members three hours a
day.

But I am not a priest. And I'm not a psy-
chologist. And I don't have many answers to
the problems I find myself immersed in on the
street.

I'm just this guy who drives a van. And if
you call me, I'll come and be with you. And if
you're hungry I'll give you a sandwich. And if

you're thirsty I'll give you something to drink. And if you want shelter, I'll try to find it for you. And if you're in Juvenile Hall, the chaplain can get me in to see you.

The little girl in front of me probably didn't know this is scripture, and that's ok.

My hope for each kid I meet on the street is my hope for myself: a long and enriching life. Somewhere down the line maybe they'll read scripture themselves and remember the big blue van on Hollywood Boulevard. Maybe not.

In training at the Covenant House Faith Community on 8th Avenue in New York, we were told: "*You* may be the only gospel one of our kids ever reads."

When I am on the street for Covenant House, talking to kids, I represent and am beholden to the boundless love and inspiring faith of a hundred thousand Californians. Many of these people support Covenant House not just financially, but with prayers of their own.

The prayers of our friends and supporters give our kids the strength and the grace to go on when they have no strength left of their own, and no apparent reason to try.

Such prayers have also kept my co-workers
and me safe from harm all these nights. I could
not search for a child in an abandoned building
teeming with crazed crack addicts and gang
members if I didn't *know* good people were
praying for us all over California. I couldn't do
it. I wouldn't do it. And they give me strength
and faith to overcome the defense mechanism
bitterness of scared little girls like this one.

Someone should write a prayer for our
kids, for this girl. Some combination of words
and images that expresses her young inno-
cence, the desperate sadness and longing for
love that wails almost inaudibly behind her anger and her sarcasm, and the thick "coolness"
that suggests everything is fine and she'd rather
be left alone.

A prayer that suggests even a glimmer of
the love that lies waiting for her in heaven, a
love she has deserved to know all her life.

A prayer to remind me that until these kids
get to heaven and God engulfs them with His
love, we are called to shower them with ours.

"Are you, like, affiliated with Christ in any
way?" she wanted to know.

"No more than most people," I smiled.

"Oh," she said, unexpectedly disarmed. She took my Covenant House card and looked back at me. "My name is Stray," she said.

Is a 53 "lib Shep

SOME HELPFUL READING

If you know a parent of a teenager who needs extra help, you may want to recommend these books (of course, our NINELINE counselors are always ready to help, and just a free phone call away—1-800-999-9999).

Buntman, Peter H., M.S.W., ACSW, and Eleanor M. Saris, M. Ed. *How to Live With Your Teenager: A Survivor's Handbook for Parents*, (New York: Ballantine, 1979).

Ginott, Dr. Haim G. *Between Parent and Teenager* (New York: Avon Books, 1971).

Kolodny, Dr. Robert C. and Nancy, and Dr. Thomas E. Bratter and Cheryl Deep. *How to Survive Your Adolescent's Adolescence* (Boston: Little & Brown, 1984).

Smith, Manual J., Ph.D. *Yes, I Can Say No: A Parent's Guide to Assertiveness Training for Children* (New York: Arbor House, 1986).

Youngs, Bettie B. *Helping Your Teenager Deal with Stress: A Parent's Survival Guide* (Los Angeles: Jeremy Tarcher, 1986).

Chapter 6

"You guys are a *joke.*" Edgar said. "Why did I even call you guys? Why did I even bother to get my hopes up? Stop handing out these dumb cards. You're just a sandwich van." He walked slowly away, shaking his head.

We'd been working with Edgar on the street for a month, convincing him over time that he was worth more than the forty dollars he got for his flesh on Santa Monica Boulevard. Edgar called us when Alan, his friend and fellow male prostitute, tested HIV positive. "Kevin, take me out of here," he said, "come pick me up." And then we couldn't find him a bed anywhere in L.A..

The card I handed out every night read, "Need someone who really cares about you? A safe place? We're here to help." L.A.'s lack of shelter beds had made me a liar too many

times. Nineline calls from kids had become a
sore spot, a wound that was touched every time
the phone rang.

When we first got to L.A., Covenant
House didn't have a shelter of its own yet. We
were still trying to find property on which to
build our crisis center. All we had were the
vans, an office, and six street staff. When a kid
asked us for a place to stay, we would call
every shelter in the city. The shelter workers
would get mad at us.

"*You just called two hours ago!* We were
full then, and *we're still full.* Have him try in
the morning at nine a.m. when the intake
worker is here."

Great, I thought. At nine a.m. when the sun
is up and it's safe, he'll be in a cheap motel
room, or asleep under a bush in Plummer Park
like everybody else. This wasn't about a place
to sleep. It was about acting on Edgar's decision to leave the street, giving him hope that a
life beyond this nasty, life-threatening trade of
sex for money was possible.

Now I was on my way to talk to a kid
named Ray in a parking lot on Sunset and Poin-
settia. Ray would be our third turn-away tonight. It was only eleven p.m..

"Aw, geez," I kept mumbling to myself. "Ugh." I wanted to jump out of the van at every stoplight and just walk away.

The grocery parking lot was deserted. John circled a few times, then parked the van in a conspicuous spot. Sometimes we get calls like this and the kids change their minds, never come. "We'll give him until 11:20," John said. I looked at the clock: five after. I *hoped* he wouldn't come.

"I'm not going to let you find him," God said.

It was *my* voice, clearly, in my head. But it wasn't something I was thinking and not the sort of thing I usually say to myself. I guess it could've been my conscience, or a part of me that knew better and finally decided to speak up, but it still scared me.

"Not with that *attitude. I'm not going to let you find him."*

Hmm. I looked over at John to see if he thought I was acting strangely. He was humming along with a song on the radio, calmly scanning the parking lot for some sign of Ray.

"Listen," the voice went on, paternal but annoyed. "I put you here. And I did so for a reason. And you are *not* in charge. I will never give you a problem without giving you the answer. It may not be the answer you want, and it may not be easy to find, but it will *be there. So shut up and do your job.!''*

Wow. Okay.

As I silently gave in, John pointed, "There he is!"

Ray was running toward us, out of breath. He was a tall, husky kid. He looked like a high school football player running off the field after a long game. When he got in the van, he smelled like one.

"I haven't slept since you saw me three days ago," he said. "I've been thinking since we talked. I gotta do something. I can't live out here anymore . . ."

I didn't know what to do. There were no more answers in my head than before, just this idea, that I *wanted* to believe, that there was an answer.

"Call the welfare shelter on Vine," John said.

I already called them, they said they were full, I wanted to say. But I shut up and dialed.

"James, this is Kevin again in the Covenant House van," I began apologetically. "Listen, I don't mean to harass you, my friend; but I've got another guy here and I'm wondering if you have anything at all you can throw my way, half a room, anything."

"Weeell, lessee," James said. I heard rustling papers. "One of my guys didn't show up for eleven o'clock curfew. I'll give you his bed."

Ray called through the Nineline three days later to thank us. After a long talk and some phone work the next morning, Micheline had put him on a bus to Marin County, California. He was working in his mom's boyfriend's hardware store. "We're talkin' again, me and her," he said.

As time went on, Covenant House added more staff and services. Now we even have our own shelter. We couldn't wait two years to find and buy property on which to build our large crisis center and residence. We couldn't bear telling kids there was nowhere to go. We now lease a building on Sunset Boulevard near Western where our kids can stay. Though it's very small, it allows us to shelter 45-plus kids who would otherwise be on the street.

Edgar, the kid who said we were just a sandwich van, was one of the first residents in our small house. But he only stayed four days.

Sometimes, the steps between life on the street and a stable, productive life are too far apart.

The second time Edgar came in he stayed one week. The third time, two weeks. Recently, after his fourth entry to our program, he moved into an apartment, with money in the bank and our blessing. He shares a small place in Hollywood with another of our former residents, and sells vitamins over the phone on commission.

It takes a lot of strength to let go of a way of life where you don't put faith in anybody or anything beyond yourself. I was confronted with this the night Edgar and Ray called us. Edgar learned it over a year of coming and going at Covenant House. We are both learning, slowly, to trust: ourselves, other people, God. The world isn't always as nasty a place as the two of us have been led to believe.

HOW TO SPEAK UP WHEN GRADES GO DOWN

Deteriorating performance in school is a problem that most parents must deal with at one point or another. Here are some tips that will help:

- **Be a friend, not an adversary.** Let your child know that you realize how hard it is to do well in school— and be ready to help. Teach him better study habits. Pump up her self-esteem. And have him tested if you suspect there may be a learning disability.

- **Look for the underlying reasons** for the poor performance. Rather than just scolding or punishing your child, try to find out *why* she's having trouble at school. Is there friction in the household? Does your child feel excluded from the social scene at school? Has he experienced the loss of a friend or relative?

- **Be realistic about your kid's capabilities.** One of the worst things a parent can do is demand more of a child than he is capable of. Not all kids can become doctors, lawyers or scientists. Perhaps she has a talent for art, music, athletics, or working with tools. Encourage your child's strengths while helping to work on the weaknesses.

Chapter 7

"Oh, take a look at *this* guy," Jana said as we cruised down Santa Monica Boulevard. We were driving slowly, scanning for young hustlers, prostitutes, like we do every night.

He was a skinny blond kid in jeans and a short-sleeved plaid shirt standing awkwardly on the corner. He looked just like the scared Midwest farm boy he turned out to be.

Lamont, an older hustler whom we've known a long time, was making fun of how *white* the kid looked. Lamont was high as a kite and had befriended the boy, probably more for his own amusement than anything else. "Hey Richie!" Lamont kept calling from several feet away. *"Richie Cunningham!"*

The young man had been in town only two days and didn't know what to do. He was trying to hustle, sell his body for hotel money.

Johns were nearly crashing into each other, stopping traffic, trying to pick him up. But he was too afraid to get into a car. *"What do I do?"* he begged Lamont in a panic. Lamont just laughed. "Call Fonzie," he said, bent over in tears, holding his stomach. "Call *The Fonz.*"

Imagine it. Exiled from all you ever had. You smell, you're hungry, your clothes are dirty, your hair is dirty and uncombed, you're sitting on a curb, and you don't know where to go.

Then a car pulls up. You are offered money for your body, money that will buy your first meal in two and a half days. You say no. Several hours and a dozen no's later you're too hungry, and too tired to care anymore.

For some of our kids, it comes down to hustling or suicide. Life usually wins, but not always.

Will power can stave off exhaustion and hunger for only so long. Our kids survive, then, by using their two remaining assets: their young bodies and the human ability to do unpleasant things and avoid seriously thinking about them, for a while.

Most of the kids we meet had never previously been involved in such things before they found themselves homeless. Many expressed revulsion at the thought of prostituting. Still, many kids don't think they have a choice.

So, you sell your body for money so you can eat and sleep in a cheap motel with all the *other* hustlers. Now you're even more of a pariah. You're not just homeless now. You are also a prostitute.

Your "friends" and fellow hustlers are too often people like Lamont. When pressed, they are only concerned about their own survival and at best, even under the smiles, are simply cautious and temporary allies. One afternoon when you wake up, Lamont, and half your clothes, will be gone.

The "johns," your customers, are liars who will say anything if it will help them steal some of the beauty, youth and natural grace of a young boy or girl. They are decrepit vampires who drink the blood of the young to briefly glow with the life and youth so sickly absent in themselves. It cruelly drains you in a very real way.

After a short while you've changed so much you can no longer picture yourself sitting around the dinner table at home. "If Mom saw me now . . ."

If a kid discovers us or we discover a kid in time, we can save them. A lot of experienced people, like the police and other agencies that deal with runaway kids, say that if somebody doesn't get to these kids before they're on the street two weeks, it's too late to save them.

But the boy Jana had noticed was a new face to me, and set off alarms in my head that said, "It's not too late!"

His name was Jim. We got him into the van and away from the old men leering and Lamont's jeering. We drove way down Curson, almost to Fountain, and stopped to talk.

"My dad threw me out," Jim said, "because I was gay."

"I came home and all my stuff was scattered on the lawn. My dad threw it out of my window on the second floor. He was still throwing it out. He yelled at me through the window. 'Get off of my lawn, you faggot! You're not my son, you goddam faggot!' Some neighbors were there. My brother called up his friends. They were sitting on the front steps with a case of beer, laughing, waiting for me."

"My brother is a *drug addict*! He used to steal stuff from the house and sell it. My dad always let him back, paid thousands of dollars for hospital rehabilitation that didn't work. My brother never finished high school. *But he's got a girlfriend.* My graduation is tomorrow! They're going to call my name and I'm not going . . ."

He broke down. Tears streamed down his red face. Tears of shame, of rage.

This kid, who played varsity basketball and worked weekends and summers at a gas station near his house, had been a good son all his life, had tried to be, and had thought he was.

Now all of that seemed a lie, a deception. Suddenly, Jim wasn't really a good student, he wasn't intelligent, or considerate, or an excellent athlete. He wasn't worthy of college, a career in professional sports or business, a place in his family, or the love of his parents. He wasn't a good son. He never had been. He deserved to live on the street. He was a faggot.

Jim covered his face with his hands, sobbing, convulsing.

Lord, what kind of job is this that you have given me, I thought, where I pull up in a van, say hello, and within minutes courageous young people, braver by far than I can ever hope to be, crumble and weep like infants, convinced that they are garbage?

Depending on how long they've had to survive out here, and how it's made them feel inside, some kids respond to our van with fury or caution. But others, like Jim, cast themselves upon our mercy, surrender to us, commend themselves into our hands, almost instantly.

At first it is overwhelming. At times the responsibility is draining. But it is *always* extraordinary: the idea that *we are good people*. On these street, where "friends" like Lamont are a dime a dozen, genuine concern and trustworthiness is water in the desert. And kids can sense it.

It happens often. Kids like Jim tell us they were straining, ready to crack, on the verge of collapse, and then we drove by, saw them, and stopped. It's close to a miracle, they say. And I believe it. I never get used to it. You'd feel it yourself if you rode with us only one night.

IF YOU ARE A PARENT STRUGGLING WITH A TROUBLED CHILD, REMEMBER . . . .

- Parents are people too.
- Parents' material and emotional resources are limited.
- Blaming keeps people helpless.
- Kids' behavior affects parents.
- Parents' behavior affects kids.
- Taking a stand precipitates a crisis.
- From controlled crisis comes positive change.
- Families need to give and get support in their own community in order to change.

Chapter 8

You're here again tonight, and I'm kind of glad, though I'm not letting on. I don't want you to get too cocky. I don't want you to think, like, that I need Covenant House in any way. I like seeing you guys, you probably know this, but it's a casual thing, really. It's not such a big deal.

At three a.m. a cool wind washed over everyone on Hollywood Boulevard, briefly lifting the thick blanket of heat and summer malaise. Stray's death phase, with its requisite funeral attire, dyed hair and black lipstick was long past now. Sitting casually against the wall of Tomy's Burgers in a light brown tank top and jeans, resting her elbows on the sidewalk, the little girl, now seventeen, talked on and on.

It was unlike her, perhaps brought on by
the cool respite, or walking too long alone on
dusty streets. This one time only, in a friend-
ship characterized by unspoken understanding
and silent respect, a pressure valve inside Stray
opened and calmly issued steam: no outbursts,
just slow rises and dips in intensity for over an
hour. I can't remember what words she used.
The words were irrelevant. But what I heard
her saying between the lines was:

*"I'm enjoying talking with you guys to-
night. I like it when you're funny. Hanging out
with you when you're funny is neat, and I get to
eat your sandwiches and sometimes there's a
crowd and I have a good time. It's a lot like
hanging out at Astro Burgers, or like Oki Dogs
used to be. I like those nights.*

*"Some nights you're not funny and I don't
have so much fun. When you're not in such a
good mood I look in your eyes and I see a tired
desperation. I see what my life must look like in
your eyes and how seeing me night after night
depresses you and wears you down. Maybe you
do know what it's like out here. I mean, maybe
I don't let you in on a lot of the things I do
because I'm embarrassed or afraid you won't
like me any more. But I'm starting to think that*

you see enough. Enough to know that it's awful out here. And when you're not laughing, I can't pretend it isn't awful.

"*I want to crack jokes to make you laugh, so we can laugh together and pretend, for just one more night please, that it isn't awful. Please don't remind me, by your silence, or your eyes, or the look of cold distaste I notice when you see a street fight, or a john pick a kid up, what this life is really like.*

"*From time to time I get mad at you for reminding me, every time I see you, that maybe I would be happier if I weren't here. I'm cold to you. Or I act like everything's under control and this is just a nice social call for the two of us. It's not that I don't like you. Occasionally, for my own sanity, I have to act this way to you. But I'm glad when you come back.*

"*What I can't tell you is that I don't know what else to do. I don't know what else to do,*

"*Some nights we're both in a good mood. We're not cracking jokes or anything, but when you pull up, a look we share says 'I'm glad to see you. I'm glad to see you because we know each other. We see through each other. We don't have anything to prove to one another. Amid long hours that take us both to places*

we'd rather not be, I can relax and you can
relax.' I hop into your van and we hang. Some
of what we say is idle chatter, catching up.
Maybe we're not saying much but I've got to
tell you sitting in your van is like a vacation for
me.

"So I'm sorry if I'm a bit rough on you
sometimes. I think I try to make you mad so
you'll go away and harass some other punk.

"I never got along with my father. Why
should I think I can get along with him now?
All my friends have graduated by now. What
would my dad think if he found out the things I
did to survive out here? What would I say I
did? How am I going to explain this rash that
comes and goes?

"A job . . . I don't know if I could make it
on $4.25 an hour. To move into an apartment
around here is like a thousand bucks. I don't
even know how to find an apartment. What
would I do all night? Who would my friends
be? I wouldn't be able to hang out with you
guys any more. I don't trust anybody else. It's
not fair.

"Please don't be mad with me if I don't
want to go back to Covenant House with you.
Like you said Thursday, something in me needs

to stay out here a little longer. I didn't answer when you said that then. I was annoyed. But I've repeated that line to myself over and over for three days.

"*I may not tell you, but the more I think about going to Covenant House, the more I wish I were dead. I don't know if I want to deal with all of this crap. This is so unfair. Why did I have to wind up out here? I didn't ask to be here. I didn't say, 'Oh God, please send me to earth and please make me homeless in Hollywood.' Whenever I think about going to Covenant House again I get exhausted. I just want to lie down and go to sleep. I just want to lie down and slip into a coma. And I'll either die or somebody will find me and take me to a hospital and take care of me, and fix me up, and then everything will be fine.*"

I can only remember one line from the torrent of words that came out on the surface, and that was the last thing Stray said that night.

"By the way," she said as Robert and I got back in the van, "my real name is Lisa."

HOW WELL DO YOU KNOW YOUR KIDS?

You may say, "My teenager wouldn't do that." Most don't. But even if yours wouldn't, think about the following questions:

- Where is your child right now?
- What are your teen's deepest fears?
- Who is your son's or daughter's best friend?
- Do your teen's friends feel welcome in your home?

Remember, a strong relationship with your children is the best way for you to guide them, and to prevent them from becoming a sorry statistic.

Chapter 9

"Hi, I'm Kevin. This is Robert. We work for Covenant House. You guys ever heard of Covenant House?"

I was leaning slightly out of the van window, and I tapped at the words Covenant House on the side of the van below me.

The four boys were silent. They were about fourteen, probably heading from one kid's house to another. Two wore sweaters, two sported blue nylon jackets. The kids in blue looked like brothers, probably were.

"Listen," I continued undaunted, "if you guys know anybody who doesn't have a place to stay, say they get kicked out of their house or they run away, or they're thinking about running away, would you give them our card?" I held out a card to the nearest kid who was about five feet away. He didn't budge.

They were just staring at me, oddly, the way children stare at anthills rising between cracks in the sidewalk.

"Alright. Do me a favor. What does it mean when a phone number begins with one-eight-hundred?"

"It's free," the kid farthest to my left said. The others looked at him nervously.

I turned and directed my talk to him. "That's right, it's free. Our number is free. It's one-eight-hundred-nine-nine-nine-nine-nine-nine-nine. It's called the Nineline."

They laughed.

I laughed, too. "Anybody under twenty-one can call us any time of the day or night. You can call us, too. All right. Now what's our number?"

They smiled, embarrassed. "One-eight-hundred-nine-nine-nine-nine-nine-nine-nine . . ." They kept saying nine, looking down, laughing.

"Alright, alright, calm down. And you!" I pointed to the smaller boy in blue nylon, shyly hiding behind his brother. "You read it off the van! Cheater! Now turn around. Say it again."

He turned his back to the van. "Nine-nine . . ."

"Aaaaaaaggggggg!" A throaty game show buzzer. "I'm sorry, you don't win the car. Who's our next contestant?"

He whirled around. "Give me another chance! Another chance!"

"Should we? I don't know . . ."

"NO! NO!" his friends shouted. "He gets the home game," his brother yelled.

"Well, I wouldn't normally do this, but the studio audience is clearly behind you, so you get another chance. What's your name?"

"Fernando," he smiled.

"All right, Fernando. Turn around."

He snuck a quick peek at the numbers on the side of the van and spun around, covering his eyes. **"One -eight-hundred** . . ."

"Twelve, *three*, seven." His brother was trying to screw him up. The other kids joined in. *"Fourteen,* two, *eleven."*

"Nine-nine-nine-nine-nine-**nine-nine**!" Fernando spun back around beaming.

"Aaaand the crowd goes wild!" I shouted, and turned quickly around to Robert. "What can we give him?"

Robert ripped our mascot, a three-inch-tall plastic Bugs Bunny, off the dash and handed it to me. "This."

I whirled back around. "You win...*a three-inch-tall plastic Bugs Bunny. Yaaaaaaay!*" I handed Fernando the toy.

"Hey, what do *I* get?" His brother demanded.

"You get the home game," I said, handing him a card.

He stared at the card for a second. "Hey, if somebody was like, gettin' hit by their father, could they call you?"

The other kids got quiet.

"Of course. Yes. I *want* them to call us. I *want* to talk to them. We help a lot of kids that happens to. Does that happen to you?"

"No," he said.

"Do you have a friend that happens to?" I asked, probing. "Let's talk about it."

But he wouldn't. "I just wanted to know," he said.

I reconsidered them for a second. "Do you guys have a place to stay?"

"Yeah. We live right over there." Fernando's brother pointed down Edgemont. He said the address. To prove it, I guess.

"Well, it's getting late. You ought to get home." I gave them all a few Covenant House cards. "It was nice meeting you guys. My name is Kevin. What was *your* name?" I extended my hand to Fernando's brother.

"Miguel. Michael."

"Nice to meet you, Miguel." I shook his hand, then the other two.

"Ralph."

"Jorge."

"You guys know our number," I reminded them. "God knows you can never forget it now. Don't forget what it's for. Call anytime. Ask for me or Robert if you want. And tell anybody you think ought to know. This is your job now. I'm making all of you deputy outreach workers. And if you see the van again, wave us down. We'll play Wheel of Fortune. Deputy Fernando will win again."

Fernando smiled.

"No way. You shouldn't have given him another chance," the others said. We drove on. "Nine-nine-nine-nine-nine . . ." they called after us, laughing.

HOW TO TALK TO YOUR TEEN ABOUT SEX

Start by admitting your anxiety. It's natural to be a little nervous. By admitting your feelings, you start the conversation off on a note of honesty and candor.

Don't try to be an expert. You're not supposed to be Masters and Johnson. Talk about your own teenage years —your feelings and experiences—to get your teen talking.

Team up with your spouse. Kids are fascinated by the details of their parents' early romance. Start talking about yourselves casually, and the rest of the discussion will take care of itself.

Don't make agreement your goal. The purpose of any parent-teenager discussion is to share information, ideas and feelings, not to achieve agreement on every issue. Don't pry or accuse.

Teach the difference between love and sex. Too many kids (and adults) confuse sex and love. Tell your kids that sex without love is wrong.

Give them a book you can discuss together. There are lots of good books about sex. Find one you feel comfortable with—make sure it is age-appropriate and reflects your religious and moral convictions. Give it to your teen and talk about it later.

Chapter 10

As usual, Stray's request for help began with a reiteration of how much she *didn't* need Covenant House. Our van was just off Hollywood Boulevard, passing out hot chocolate and sandwiches in front of an alley some kids sleep in. Three mildewed mattresses interrupted the drift of city street trash that lined one wall. Against the other wall a rusty green dumpster, half full, eaves open, rustled with unseen rodents.

Twirling her long auburn hair around a thin finger, Stray cited the great things street life offered her, "I don't have to deal with my parents; I don't have to go to school; I don't have to do any work; I don't have a curfew; I can have a boyfriend; I can do what I want. On the street, I've got no responsibilities."

is that what we really want

"I have responsibilities," I said. "I have a job. I do this. And I <u>love</u> it. I wouldn't do anything else right now. Just because something's a job doesn't mean you have to hate it."

She wrinkled her forehead, unconvinced. It was a new concept for her.

"What job would you take if you could do anything you wanted?" I asked.

"I like animals," she said. "I'd like a job working with animals."

Of course she would, I thought, smiling. She could love them and they would never let her down. Even if they did, say by getting run over, it wouldn't be their fault. They were innocent. They were victims, like her.

Then it dawned on me. *Stray*, her street name, it was perfect.

"I'm starving," she admitted as we walked to the van to join the group of kids eating and joking with Richie, my van partner. "I've got no money. I didn't eat today."

I didn't respond. I just sort of nodded and handed her a sandwich.

"I've got no place to take a shower, and these are the only pants I have. Somebody stole all my stuff again. I've gotta start with nothing, *again*. My best friend Maria bailed on me and took off to Colorado with some dude who got her into crack. Now he pimps her. My squat burned down and I haven't found a new abandoned building yet. Well, I found one and went inside but these two guys already lived there and started hunting me all over the building, saying they were going to rape me, yelling out all the things they were going to do to me when they found me. The things they were describing echoed all over the building. I was trapped up on the fourth floor. I hid in this hole in the floor where someone had ripped out a toilet. I closed my eyes, like I was a little kid, like, if I couldn't see them, they couldn't see me . . . ."

She stopped speaking. It wasn't because she was finished, but because her casual facade had collapsed. The emotions she'd been suppressing for so long finally welled up and drowned her words. She closed her mouth and looked hesitantly at me. I didn't learn the rest of the story.

"Nobody should have to live like that," I said honestly.

Stray looked quickly away. Was the truth too much right now?

"Come to Covenant House. Please, Stray. You can come tonight. You can come right now. There's a place for you there. It doesn't have to be this way."

Stray wouldn't look at me. She stared quietly at the corner of the dumpster, I saw a single tear trace a thin shiny line from her eye to her chin. She wiped it away with the sleeve of her large blue sweatshirt.

"Just try it," I said to reassure her. "If you don't like it you can leave. This alley will always be here . . . Can we at least talk about it?"

She waved her head almost imperceptibly from side to side. No.

"Ok." I sighed, conceding. "I'll look for information on jobs with animals, Lisa." I slid back into my seat. "I'll have it the next time I see you." I closed the van door and rolled down my window. "I worry about you. I know you don't want me to, and I know you don't want to hear about it. But I do. Please, *take care of yourself.*"

Richie backed the van slowly out of the alley, careful for kids who might be rounding the corner from Cherokee. He straightened out and shifted into forward, ready to move on. I glanced sideways towards Stray, who was watching me.

"I always have," she said.

HOW TO WIN YOUR
TEEN'S COOPERATION

Always try to understand what your child is feeling.

You don't have to agree or condone to understand. If possible, share an example of a time when you felt the same.

Share your feelings about the situation in a non- accusing manner. Children are willing to hear you after they feel heard.

Work together on ideas to avoid the problem in the future—or to correct the present problem through a logical consequence.

If the first three steps have been done in a respectful manner, your child will be ready for cooperation in the fourth step.

Chapter 11

get babies drunk :: sleep

"When I was a baby, my dad used to put Jack Daniels in my bottle in little baby portions so I'd get drunk and not wake up or cry while he slept at night."

Through the curtain of his long blonde hair, Bitter's bloodshot, exhausted brown eyes looked sea-green. His once athletic frame had melted over the last four months. Emaciated and nervous, he slouched in the van seat, staring at me.

Bitter's dad was an alcoholic. Bitter was recovering. His real name is Matt. When he was fifteen and the beatings became too frequent and too savage, Matt ran away. He then systematically exhausted the charity of his relatives. After a while, they could no longer locate their drunk brother, and they didn't really want to raise his son. They kept passing him along.

One day his Uncle Steve handed him a ticket from Indiana to Ohio. "You can stay there for the summer. At your Aunt Marion's," he said.

Matt's aunt wasn't at the station when his bus pulled into Dayton at 7 a.m. He called but there was no answer. He hitched to her house but found it locked. He waited on the porch steps. At noon, a neighbor came to take junk mail from his aunt's box.

"They're in Maine for the summer. Been gone three weeks. Won't be back for eight more," she said.

Matt broke into the house. On his third day the neighbor let herself in to water the plants. She found things moved, saw him asleep upstairs, and called the police.

His aunt, when phoned, didn't press charges. But she declined to speak to him, and told the police he was *not* welcome to stay.

Matt thought about calling his uncle or heading back to Indiana, but changed his mind. "I'll get out of their hair for a while," he thought. He just shuffled out of the police station: hair tousled, in his sleeping sweats and a tank top, wearing sneakers but no socks.

And so, four months later in Hollywood, he and I made some calls from the van. One aunt denied knowing him. The second said no, but gave us the number of the first. His uncle hedged. It *had* been a while. But "Nooooo. I don't think so," he said finally.

"You don't have to feed me," Matt bargained. "Just give me a blanket. I'll sleep by the stream, where I used to put the tent. *I'm not asking for anything.*" He repeated this plea four times, his face dripping with tears, before his uncle hung up on him. He handed me the phone.

This is how it happens most often to our kids. Without fanfare, without anger, without malice. A simple sin of omission on the part of his uncle and his aunts, one easily shrugged off. "How much am I expected to do for the kid? I couldn't do any more for him." Matt had been banished, exiled. There was no going back.

It was then, on the way to Covenant House in our outreach van at two in the morning, transporting a silently crying eighteen-year-old boy too shattered to be embarrassed, that the prayer came to me. The prayer I had been

searching for, for kids like Matt, for all our
kids, a prayer that speaks for them, the Salve
Regina:

Hail, holy Queen, mother of mercy,
our life, our sweetness, and our hope.
To you do we cry,
poor banished children of Eve.
To you do we send up our sighs
mourning and weeping in this valley of tears.

Turn then, most gracious advocate,
thine eyes of mercy toward us,
and after this, our exile,
show unto us the blessed fruit of thy womb,
Jesus.

O clement, O loving,
O sweet Virgin Mary.

Pray for us, O holy mother of God,
that we may be made worthy of the promises
of Christ.

Amen.

Chapter 12

"You haven't heard?" Jammer said casually. "Stray is dead. She was shot in gang crossfire down at the hotel squat four nights ago. She's gone. Dead and buried. But I'm alive. Do you have any sandwiches?"

Washed by the yellow streetlamps and perspiring under the muggy blanket of summer air, everyone on the sidewalk in front of Tomy's Burgers suddenly looked ill with hepatitis. I'd been asking for Stray, to give her a list I'd made of every animal shelter, veterinary clinic, and pet store within reasonable bus distance of Hollywood.

I stood numbly at the door to the burger place, staring at the door knob, its image slowly burning into my mind. Without thinking I reached down, opened my bag, and gave Jammer a sandwich.

What am I doing here? I thought, standing on the muggy sidewalk. I can't do this any more. I don't want to do this any more. I was gripped by the desire to get in the van and drive away, to another city, one kids don't run to, like Wyoming, and work on a farm or something until I stopped seeing their faces when I closed my eyes.

I'd watched too many kids go under out here, telling themselves they weren't worth the lifeline I was throwing them. I felt the love inside of me, the very force that dragged me into this work, being slowly murdered by the same despair and hopelessness that robs the kids of their love and youth and hope and self-worth.

The same despair that kept Stray on these streets despite our offers of help. The same despair that drove her to sleep in the abandoned building, where, the kids say, she was shot twice in the chest and once in the arm, dying before the ambulance arrived.

In time, I would grieve. In time, I would be able to pray for Lisa, for "Stray", confident that her exile was at last over. In time, I would be able to give again, to feel for kids in pain at the risk of being hurt again myself. But standing there, in front of Tomy's, staring at that doorknob, I felt nothing at all.

Chapter 13

"It's been a month since we called my uncle, Kevin. Since I came to Covenant house. I forgot what it was like on the street. You've gotta find me a place to stay tonight. Tomorrow I'm going to ask Teresa if I can get back in. I hope she lets me. Oh, man, she's gotta let me come back."

An hour before, in an argument over the last piece of chocolate cake, Matt had stormed out of Covenant House saying it was an awful place and he was never coming near it again.

Then, at the door of the abandoned building he used to stay in, an older junkie shooting heroin said, "Hey, Bitter. S'up, Dude? Slam with me, man. Stuff's good. Cheap, too. Show me your cash, man. Step right this way." Matt turned and headed back to Covenant House.

But another kid had arrived to claim Matt's bed before it was even cold.

One of the most important lessons we teach kids in transition from the streets is this: behavior has consequences. Matt had lost his bed.

But we didn't want to see Matt back on the street after a month of progress, either. As a van worker, I was prepared to find him an alternate place to stay for the night, to give him a safe time and place to consider his behavior. Then, when he returned to Covenant House remorsefully in the morning, he'd get his bed back with a lecture.

Usually, Matt, as his street alter-ego Bitter, bounced around Covenant House with his long blonde hair flying, like it was an MTV video set. Now he looked forlorn, chewing on his lower lip as I checked the van's oil in the shelter driveway, "Come on, Kevin. I've got nowhere else to go!"

"Relax," I assured him. "Let's talk. Tell me, Matt, what was your plan this time through Covenant House?"

"The Army. I was supposed to go in tomorrow morning. I guess I blew *that*, huh?"

So that was it. I knew there had to be more to his storming out than a piece of chocolate cake. "I can find you a place to stay tonight, Matt." I said, slamming the hood. "Of course I can. But a place to stay isn't your problem. *Sabotage* is your problem."

"I don't take pills."

"Sabotage isn't a drug, Matt. It's fear." I looked at him squarely. "Ok. What was your plan the *last* time through Covenant House?"

"I was going to get an apartment. I got a job and saved a thousand dollars."

"What happened?"

"I bought an electric guitar and an amplifier."

"Where are they now?" I asked.

"Some junkie in the squat stole them for crack."

I thought for a moment, then turned to him baffled. "Matt, was there *electricity* in the squat?"

"No." he admitted.

"Where did you play your guitar, then?"

"I don't know how. I was going to take lessons. But I lost my job."

"Because you didn't have a place to stay," I guessed.

"I *did*," he insisted. "I was living in the *squat*. I didn't have an alarm clock."

They were dumb moves, but dumb with brilliant precision. "Look at the pattern, Matt," I implored him. "You do fine. You do fine because there's no reason not to do fine. You're a good guy with a heart of gold. But just before it's all about to come together and pay off for you, you bail, you go back to the street. Tell me, what goes on in your gut when you think about going into the Army in the morning?"

"But I'm not going. I blew it," he shrugged helplessly.

"But say you hadn't..," I pressed him.

"I don't know." He opened and closed his fist. "I . . ."

He was caught between two worlds, like so many of our kids. He doesn't really have a family. He's old enough now that nobody but the military is willing to take care of him.

But Matt's eighteen. He's just a kid. He wants to be happy, to learn the guitar, to have a girlfriend. He doesn't really want to live in a barracks and learn how to be a soldier.

He just wants to be a kid a little longer. He never really got to enjoy it. Now he's told he has to be an adult. He was robbed, and he feels robbed.

I secured Matt a bed in a small welfare hotel near Covenant House. He slept there, and met his recruiter on our steps in the morning.

It's hard for me to push a kid whom life has shoved so much already. Too often, in the face of this ineffable suffering, which none of us at Covenant House can explain, we need to convince Matt and hundreds of other kids like him that it is best if they go one step further, and impose suffering upon themselves.

They must sacrifice much pleasure, much independence, and ultimately much of their youth if they're going to make it. They have to get their diplomas, find jobs, even join the army, when they'd rather just lay down on the sand of this urban desert and let the winds bury them, when they'd rather just quit, when they have every right to, when I probably would if I were in their place.

Matt's got a couple of things going for him: We love him, and he knows it. And God loves him, and he knows it.

Elijah went a day's journey into the desert, until he came to a broom tree and sat beneath it. He prayed for death: "This is enough, O Lord! Take my life, for I am no better than my fathers.'' He lay down and fell asleep under the broom tree, but then an angel touched him and ordered him to get up and eat. He looked and there at his head was a hearth cake and a jug of water. After he ate and drank, he lay down again, but the angel of the Lord came back a second time, touched him, and ordered, ''Get up and eat, else the journey will be too long for you!'' He got up, ate and drank; then strengthened by that food, he walked forty days and forty nights to the mountain of God, Horeb.''

1 Kings 19:4-8

Matt called me once from a payphone at the base laundromat where he was stationed. "It's okay here," he told me. "It's not so bad." We talked for a while. I dragged out the conversation, engrossed, listening to the difference in his voice. He sounded a little more mature, a little less innocent.

Chapter 14

"Where do you hurt?" The nurse's pen poised clinically over the diagram of a person, ready to circle an arm or a leg on the Emergency Room intake form.

"Everywhere." Michael sighed.

The nurse glanced up, annoyed, but her face immediately softened. She lowered her glasses. Though we'd cleaned him up quick in the van, Michael's swollen face was again bloody from ear to ear. His crew cut was a wet red sponge. He was about eighteen, average height, a little overweight. "What did they hit you with?" she wondered.

"Everything they could find."

We saw him running towards Covenant House a block after we left the driveway. Neither Trey or I knew his name, but we'd both seen him at the hotel squat. He would take a sandwich and slip to the back of the crowd. He had heard all our little speeches about Covenant House and the dangers of the street, but avoided talking to us. Until now.

He explored the new geography of his face gingerly with the tips of his fingers.

"This guy in the squat had a gun. I saw it. I told on him. I wanted to protect the family. The guy took off. They couldn't find him, or the gun. They said I made the whole thing up. They moshed me. They mosh eighty-sixed me.

"They said we were a family, all of us kids living in the squat," he continued. "They said we were a *family*. Ouch!" He looked up. "I think my nose and my ribs are broken."

"Would you please have security take a police report from him?" Trey asked the nurse. The wide, off-green corridors of County Hospital were quiet tonight, so they'd probably get to him in eight hours instead of twelve or fourteen.

The automatic E.R. door slid quickly open and an orange-clad paramedic swept by with a man on a gurney. Bloody gauze was strapped to the patient's forehead. "This one's dead," the paramedic said to the nurse as he passed.

Trey turned to Michael. "You'll be fine, just take a seat."

Michael couldn't take his eyes off the curtain beyond which the dead body had been wheeled. He backed up nervously, crouched, and felt behind him for a chair.

"Ah, not in that one!" Trey cried, pointing to the chair. "There's blood all over the legs. Sit in this one."

Michael sat nervously two chairs over.

"Here's our number and a bunch of quarters," I said, handing Michael some change. "The black and white striped line will lead you to the candy machines. Make a right where it splits. When you're done here, call us. We'll come pick you up."

"Okay." He'd be fine, but looked lonely on a row of grey metal chairs by himself, all bloody and sad.

We left. "They said we were family," I repeated to myself as we climbed into the van. Removed from parental custody as an infant due to neglect, Michael had never had a family. He'd been raised in dozens of institutions, cuddled through childhood in the concrete arms of the state.

His social worker stopped checking up at his last group home shortly before he turned seventeen. At eighteen, having secured his General Equivalency Diploma, he was told he was free to go. So he left.

For a boy with this history, drifting anchorless and alone, "family" is a powerful, mythical word. I'm sure Michael heard it from the kids in the squat and thought it was a dream come true.

But for most of the guys I knew in that abandoned building, putting somebody in the hospital over something stupid is all too consistent with their experience of family.

The hotel squat is a four story, half-burned, half-renovated labyrinth of homeless kids. Some doors open to cavernous four-story drops, some rooms and hallways have weak floors. At night it is black inside. Though there are sometimes sixty denizens, none of these danger spots are marked. You have to know. If you don't know, you probably aren't welcome.

The squat is a microcosm of humanity. There are the best rooms, shared among those with influence, and the rooms the kids who are new or different get stuck with. In isolated and

foul sections of the building, human waste
stews to the brims of toilets which haven't
flushed in years. Where do the kids think it is
going to go? But going outside is a long dangerous expedition in the middle of the night.

Such abandoned buildings lie dormant, become active, are busted by the police, lie dormant, and become active again. The van staff
surfs these trends.

At night we park the van and slip through a
large slash clipped in the chain-link fence that
surrounds the block long building. We begin
our chant, "Covenant House . . . .Covenant
House . . . .Covenant House . . . ," as we cross
the large dark parking lot, nearing the
building.

Nothing.

Then a long human whistle from the kid on
watch. All clear.

Kids begin pouring from windows and
doors and the basement. They converge on us
and our waiting sandwiches.

These kids live in the worst conditions we
ever see, but unlike many kids we work with,
they have each other.

They *are* family, not always a loving one,
or a dependable one, or even a safe one, but to

most it's more of a family than they have ever known.

Any of them would be better off with us. But when I go out in the van night after night with my well-refined litany of ways we can help, most of the kids assume I simply can't be talking about them. They take a sandwich, say thanks, and walk back into their abandoned building.

To these kids, even a place as caring as Covenant House represents a system which, after repeated failures and refusals, they believe can't really help them, or doesn't really want to.

We come here anyway, and feed them, and repeat our offer of shelter and help because our love is not based on their opinion of us. And because if we don't, we will be showing them more of what they've already heard: you are unworthy, there is no love for you in this world. We come because someone has got to break the cycle, and if we don't, who will? And because every few trips, somebody from this crowd decides to take us up on our offer.

Returning to the hospital at the end of our shift, we found Michael sitting on the same chair he'd been in over seven hours earlier.

The only change was a Snickers wrapper and an empty Coke can on the seat next to him.

"He'll be seen in a little while," the nurse said.

"I think, maybe, when I'm through here, I'd like to go to Covenant House," Michael said, "if that's ok with you."

Chapter 15

"I can't believe you stayed with him!" Bobbi cursed Tiffany.

"Whoa. What's this all about?" I asked, startled.

"Her!" Bobbi yelled, pointing to Tiffany. "She left me to die!"

"Please, calm down," I asked. "What happened?"

"Last night this trick picked us both up and took us to this house in Los Feliz. As soon as we walked into the house he started pulling my hair. I told him to stop! He started clawing me with his sharp fingernails. He was ripping my shirt. He *clawed my skin!"*

Bobbi pointed to her left shoulder and I turned on the bright overhead cabin lights. She squinted. Part of her shoulder was covered with some kind of fleshtone make-up, but in this light I could clearly see a human claw mark a few inches long at the base of her neck. I also saw a rip in her lip that hadn't shown in the dim yellow street lights.

"That's nasty," Debbie said. "Wash it out good every day. Keep it clean."

"Feel my skull," Bobbi said. There was a big lump just above her ear.

"He hit me with a paperweight, a big rock. I laid on the floor. I pretended to be unconscious. He left the room to get something . . . a rope, a gun, I don't know. I didn't want to find out."

"Where were *you*?" I asked Tiffany. She sat nervously and sipped her hot chocolate.

"She was right there! In the room! Watching! She just sat there, like now, doing nothing! I said, 'Let's get out of here!' She wouldn't get up. I opened the window and jumped out. I fell ten feet into a bush and rolled down a hill. The guy set some vicious dog after me from the front door. 'Get her. Get her.' I jumped over this black iron fence with spikes on it. It was so tall. I don't know how I got over it."

Bobbi ran half-naked and bleeding down Hillhurst Street, trying to flag someone down.

No one stopped until a taxi drove by. Where could she go? She drove back to Santa Monica and Formosa, the corner. "Stop here. Now."

The taxi stopped short in the middle of the empty street. Norma, a fellow prostitute, walked into the middle of the street, opened the door, took Bobbi, and paid the driver. Norma cleaned her up, paid for her hotel room, then went back to the boulevard.

"Whoa," I sighed. I was speechless.

"I can't believe you stayed there with him," Bobbi spat at Tiffany.

"Well he *liked* me," Tiffany said finally, in her defense. "There was something about you *he just didn't like.*" Her words were immediately drowned by a silence that flooded the van. The pressure rose in the small space between the four of us, pushing on me, pushing against the inside walls of the van, I drew a shallow breath. Tiffany looked off to one side.

They sat in the van, staring at the backs of the chairs in front of them, not speaking. They'd be working together tomorrow. I knew it. Debbie knew it. They knew it.

Later, when Bobbi was gone, Tiffany would break down and in choking tears admit that she'd been confused, in shock, and too ter-

rified to come to Bobbi's aid. In less than an
hour she would be racked with guilt, seeking
understanding, begging forgiveness. But now,
in front of Bobbi, under this choking pressure,
again too weak to respond, Tiffany sat in stony
defiance: *This is the way it is. Deal with it.*

Bobbi is tired of her creepy patrons and the
hassling police, fed up with macho pimp
wanna-bees and the numbing *boredom* of
working a street-corner, tired of being strung
out on crack and selling herself cheap to buy it,
tired of getting into almost any car when the
honed instincts of another hustler would
scream, "No! He's dangerous!" But she isn't
tired enough to leave it all behind.

I can't trust these people, her face said as
she sat silently beside Tiffany, *They are not my
friends. But if I don't stay with them, I'll be
alone. The world is a big and scary place. I'd
rather be hurt than be alone.*

It is hell here, but it's a hell Bobbi knows
the rules to. The thought of Covenant House,
with the other kids, the structure, the curfew,
and all the subtle rituals of human interdepen-
dence we take for granted, terrifies her.

How bad will things have to get, I wondered, before Bobbi finds the courage to leave

this predictable awful life and come to a better, though initially unknown and unpredictable one, at Covenant House.

"You two deserve better than this." Debbie said aloud.

Chapter 16

"What are you doing here? I thought you left all this behind!"

"I did. I did. I swear. I'm just hanging out with my friends."

Ray had hustled on Santa Monica Boulevard for two months when he first arrived from New Jersey. Then he got a job fixing cars at a garage on Vine.

I parked in the driveway of a medical building near Curson and hopped out so I could read him the riot act.

"Listen you," I said, "I know you like these guys. I like them, too; but they'll drag you down. They're still on the street and you're not. They're out here peddling their tail, getting high. You ought to be home watching t.v. or something. Come on, man, you're smarter than this."

"No *you* listen," he insisted, standing taut like a boxer at the bell, "I sit at home and I watch t.v. and I'm *climbing the walls*. I walk circles in this tiny apartment listening to a friggin' *transistor radio*. I'm goin' *crazy* in there. These are my only friends, and *you-will-cut-me-some-slack!*"

"All right, so we've both got a point," I conceded brusquely, "But think about what I'm saying."

He chewed vengefully on a sandwich, gulped down some punch and ripped off another bite. *"And a mobber shing,"* he began, still chewing and pointing his finger at me.

Round two was interrupted by two short honks and a the sound of a car coming to a fast stop along the sandy curbside. I turned. A figure was stepping out of a private security car behind me. A tall, skinny, blond guy in a uniform with a big smile on his face.

"Hey," I said, my mind racing for his name. Three months ago, just feet from here, we'd met for the first time. All I could remember was Richie Cunningham. That was what Lamont had been calling him. He walked up and I shook his hand. "Look at you! . . . Jim, It's good to see you."

"Hey," he answered, and then again, "Hey," as he recognized Ray and shook his hand.

"So you went the other way on us," Ray said, mocking.

"Huh?" Jim squinted back, then looked at his chest. "Oh, the uniform..."

"You're a rent-a-cop."

"I've got a great job," he said, pointing to his patrol car, "I drive around in my unit all night, and I get to..."

"My unit," Ray snickered.

"It's a good job!" Jim protested. "And I don't have to prove *anything to you.*"

"Relax, relax. *I'm* proud of you," Jana said.

I agreed. And he's proud of himself, I thought, which is beautiful. After four days at Covenant House, he'd found a job working overnight security for a well-known company. They sent him all over L.A., a different post every night, filling in for guys who called in sick at the last minute. Sometimes the bus ride was an hour and a half each way with two transfers, in a city he didn't know.

After six weeks at Covenant House, he found a small apartment with no move-in fee.

He kept at the job. It paid off. Somebody there noticed he was a good guy with a high school diploma. They put him in a patrol car. Now he checks up on all those goldbricks he used to fill in for.

"Now I have a job driving around all night just like you guys," he said, beaming.

"I have a license," Ray interrupted. "*I* can work for the Covenant House. *I* can hand out sandwiches."

Jana and I reflected on our degrees in Social Work and Psychology, respectively. "Stick with fixing cars," Jana said flatly, "You'll get paid more."

Jim smiled, "Hey, I'm having a party Saturday. I want you guys to come."

"Oh, that's sweet, thank you;" Jana said, "but we can't. We're staff."

"That's a dumb rule," Jim smirked, but he didn't push, he understood. Then a bit too casually, he said, "My father told my sisters and my brothers that as far as he's concerned, I was never born. I can't call them. He hangs up." He paused, looking away momentarily. "I miss them. But I'm making a new family. I wanted you to be in it."

"We'll be godparents," I said quietly, looking at my sneakers.

Chapter 17

There was a ghost at the shelter door.

I was on the phone with two brothers calling from Orange County. They'd been living in a little tent hidden among shrubs off the freeway for three weeks. They'd only just heard about Covenant House. "Hold on," I said to them, and then to myself, "This isn't happening."

Stray was at the door, inexplicably alive, asking for sandwiches.

She was thin, weary, much worse for wear. But it was definitely Stray. It had been six months since we heard she'd been killed in gang crossfire at a nearby abandoned building.

"Oh. Hi, Kevin. I'm sorry to bother you, man." She was embarrassed and looked at the desk rather than me. She figured nobody at the shelter would know who she was. Only the van team knew her.

Things must be really bad, I thought. She's always been too proud to come to the door here.

"Do you have any sandwiches?" she mumbled sheepishly. "It's okay if you don't, but I'm starvin' like Marvin, man."

"Come in. Come in, Lisa," I gestured towards a couch. Where had she been? What was wrong? My God, I was so glad she was alive. "Have a seat. I'll heat you up a late dinner. We had turkey tonight." I said this with faith that our wonderful Chef Stan McKibbins had again provided surplus dinners for our stragglers, and on further faith that our stragglers hadn't eaten them all yet. "Come in, relax," I asked Lisa.

"Oh, no. No thanks, man. I'd rather not."

"It's good to see you, Lisa." I didn't know what to say.

"Oh, what a joke," she coughed.

Another kid standing there jumped in rather nervously. "Stray, I couldn't find you that day. We heard you were dead. I sold your radio. I don't have the money anymore."

"I just had to get away," Lisa groaned with a wave. "Don't worry about it."

Somebody returned with two sack lunches. Lisa took them humbly, "Thanks, man." She turned and the door sighed closed behind her.

I wanted to catch her on the sidewalk, but the brothers were still standing by their payphone in Chino, waiting to give me directions to get them in the van. Stray had slipped away.

Lisa will never understand how she can be my hero, or why I would ask God for a fraction of the strength and grace that He has granted her.

When I was younger I was inspired by men like Martin Luther King Jr., John F. Kennedy, Mohandas Gandhi. When I was a child I revered these men. Now I am a man and I revere these children.

These cold, dirty, recalcitrant street kids are an inspiration and an example to me. These kids do not have the comfort of fame. They are not lauded by anyone. They do not receive such reassuring reminders of their self-worth. They do not know that they matter, that the world *is* a better place because they are here, that this can be no less true of them than of you

or I because we were all made by the same
God.

Lisa has gone through so much pain and
betrayal and suffering and she is still standing.
She has not succumbed to the ultimate despair
of suicide as so many of her peers have. She
has taken care to stay alive in a hostile environment, and to avoid incarceration, drug addiction, Satanism and a host of other soul-numb-
ing easy exits from the reality of the streets.

Somewhere deep inside, Lisa must want to
trust and love more than anyone. Lord, *imagine the faith required,* in the face of the life
Lisa has known and knows, to hold out, to wait
for her turn, to choose to live.

Chapter 18

On Hollywood Boulevard we are often deluged
with a dozen or more hungry kids at once. It
becomes a feeding frenzy. In the rush of hands
and cups of hot chocolate, sometimes we can
only grab a new kid's name and then hand them
our card before they slip back into the crowd.

Some nights there are kids in the fray who
really want to talk. They jostle their way to the
front and say, "Kevin, I'm pregnant," or
"Kevin, I tried to kill myself yesterday." I'll be
able to get just a line in, and hope to find them
in the munching, satiated crowd spread out on
the curb a few minutes later.

And when they've talked, or listened, or
cried, they go off and walk through side streets
to think, or head back to their dark abandoned
buildings to sleep.

And when they're gone, there is always somebody left who doesn't have anything to do, who wants to stay and talk with us. Like Alex. He is very lonely, and more. He won't talk about anything really important to him yet. Still, right now we are people to whom he has told his real name, not just his street name, and who honestly like having him around.

We are not so much armed with social work theory as we are with bologna and cheese, and hot chocolate, and kindness, and respect, and a love Alex can sense is sincere when he looks in our eyes. He still cannot understand why he is worthy of our love. But he stays.

Until Alex lets us a little further into his heart, I will participate in countless irrelevant conversations about baseball, the color blue, you name it. I am willing to admit now that much of what I do is inane, consisting of long drives, getting pushed around by emergency room nurses, and talking about lint with Alex. And for this I sometimes need patience and faith.

Any every once in a while, God's grace. The phone rang. "It's for you," Jana said.

Her name was Melissa. She was calling to thank me. "You changed my life, Kevin," she said. "And I'm doing really well now. I've thought about calling to thank you about twenty times. My AA sponsor is here with me at a diner. I was talking about it again and she said, 'Well, *do it,* then.' So I am." She was out of breath, excited and nervous.

"Well that's beautiful, Melissa," I said. I wanted to ask who she was and how I'd changed her life, but I was afraid to betray my ignorance. She was so happy. But I didn't need to ask. She told me.

"You were parked in front of Tomy's Burgers on Hollywood," she said.

I looked through the windshield. I could see Tomy's only a few blocks away.

"And I was rattling on and on about all these things I was doing, and drugs I was taking, and all these boyfriends I was seeing . . . And you finally got a word in and you said, 'What are you trying not to think about that you keep yourself so busy every moment of the day?' "

"I got mad and stormed away," she said. "I never talked to you again. But is gnawed at me. Finally I sat down like two weeks later and said, 'What *am* I not trying to think about?' "

"What was it?" I asked, intrigued.

"I still don't know," she said.

"Well I'm glad I could help," I said.

She laughed. "No! No! Sitting there, I suddenly got this urge to call my mom. We hadn't talked in two years. She told me if I got clean I could come home. So I started going to the Cocaine Anonymous meetings at the West Hollywood Alcohol and Drug Center. I'm home now. Tonight, I got my one year chip at a meeting. I stood up and told everyone my story. I told them about you, too."

"That's beautiful, Melissa. Congratulations. Your call is just what I needed. Thank your sponsor for me. Tell her you made my night. But remember, you did all the work, not me."

I turned and looked at Jana and Alex. They were arguing about whether or not the heel of the bread was meant to be eaten. (Of course, Jana argues *for* the heel since it gives us one more sandwich per loaf).

How many kids have we helped without knowing it, with a word, a line, or a smile, thinking we were just biding time with inane conversation? I've gotten several almost identical calls in three years. How many kids didn't call?

Sometimes I think I'm not doing enough, that getting Alex to trust us should happen faster, that I'm not going to get a chance to help him before he, too, disappears. But now I realize our just being here is a miracle. That this is what I do, sitting here, being here, with him. That there's nowhere to go, there's nothing to do. It's happening right now, right here.

I turned back to Alex, newly content. "Okay, okay, next time we'll put mayonnaise on both sides of the bologna. I'll keep two off to the side for you. *Happy?*"

Chapter 19

I've just parked the van in the Covenant House shelter driveway, carrying two beautiful, exhausted, hungry kids who fell asleep on the ride from Venice, dreaming I'm sure, of a shower and a clean room.

"Hi, Lisa," I say as she turns to slink from the shelter with her sandwiches. She is so like a stray cat, letting us leave food at the door but refusing to come inside.

"Oh," she moans, startled. "Dude, you scared me."

"Hang out for a while," I ask her. "Talk with me. I don't see you any more."

"I'm around," she mumbles.

Lisa and I have both reached a kind of stasis in our relationship with life, the streets and each other. The highs and the lows have exhausted us and left us in the present and wary of unnecessary struggles. What energy we have we direct towards putting one foot in front of the other, reckoning as best we can with whoever and whatever presents itself.

We're both like watches now, keeping time, ticking off each second in its turn. I make a hundred sandwiches, load them into the van and head out on the streets at night looking for kids. Lisa heads out and begins asking folks for change. We know a lot, she and I. Much more than we feel the need to say in simple conversation. We both try to be good, we try not to hurt people, we help when we can, we're both happy for a day of rest when it comes.

Despite my considerable efforts, Lisa still thinks that she's just not a good person, and she doesn't deserve a better life. She thinks the street is her fate, her destiny. She's only eighteen.

A lot of experienced people, like the police and other agencies that deal with runaway kids tell me it's too late to save Lisa. She was a terminal street kid long before I ever knew what a squat was or who a john or a trick is. Too much of her soul has been eaten away, they say.

Part of me has to admit the truth of what they tell me. I'm neither blind, nor a fanatic.

Even so, I think she is better off for us having made her our own.

But I also know God can do anything He wants. And He most often needs someone to do it through. Someone willing, someone who hasn't written off any possibilities. In this case, someone who hasn't written off Lisa.

She stands nervously in the shelter driveway holding her sandwiches. She's nervous because in a transient life where her friends change every month, I've stuck around long enough to see the big picture. And the big picture isn't nearly as cool as the day to day strutting and posing that impresses the tourists and the new runaways. The big picture is actually pretty depressing, and seeing me reminds her.

"I've still got that list of animal shelters," I offer. "I won't call for you, but I'll help you with what to say, if you want."

"Maybe," she says, shuffling away. She meant it. She wasn't going to lie to me and say *sure*, like other kids might.

I find myself a chair in the backyard of our shelter to watch a bunch of former prostitutes, drug addicts, and street survivors play like kids again. About ten kids are split by a volleyball net in the sun. They're smiling, jumping to slam the ball, wiping sweat from their faces, having a good time. Others sit and talk, or read. I've helped hundreds of kids off the street in the last three years. I sit back here because this is *my* big picture, and I need to be reminded sometimes, too.

I asked Sister Mary Rose and Fred Ali for permission write this book because I wanted to thank you for all of this. And I wanted you to see, as I see, the good you do for the kids.

Epilogue

Struggling alongside kids like Lisa for twenty years, Covenant House has become a place where kids in trouble, kids with nowhere to turn, like the kids in this book, can cry for help and be rescued. A place offering the first moments of patience, compassion, understanding, and support they may encounter in their painful young lives.

For the last two years in California, we have run a small house kids can come to when they need help. They are kids nobody else has room for, and kids nobody else wants to work with. We're packed to capacity every night. We have a staff and a nurse and a clinic dedicated to meeting the many needs of our kids seven days a week.

We have this place now because we couldn't wait any longer, and God and our donors agreed. But the wait will be over soon. I'm pleased to announce that we have finally purchased property for our comprehensive Los Angeles Crisis Center.

God willing, and with the support of our donors, we will open our Covenant House Crisis Center in two more years. In our new center we will provide food, clothing, and shelter to more kids in crisis than we can right now. In addition, this center will include a floor for pregnant girls and girls with their babies, a transitional living program for kids working towards independence, an expanded health services department, and more. And it's going to be inviting, new, and clean.

Planning our center, building it, and staffing it, will take effort, time and money. Lord knows we're not short on the effort. Waiting the time required will test our patience, though. And worrying about the money has got us gnawing some pencils. But God never said it'd be easy. He just said do it.

I'd like to thank you for the love and prayers you've showered on our kids and the support you've shown Covenant House. We can only do what we do from day to day because you care. We are a humble vessel of your compassion and your faith. Our staff, our volunteer Faith Community, our kids, and I pray for you and those you love every day. Thank you, and may God bless you in all that you do.

> Fred Ali
> Executive Director
> Covenant House California

HOW YOU CAN HELP

Become politically streetwise. There are no great mysteries about it: politicians respond to appropriate, perservering pressure. There are laws that need changing and laws that need passing, like making it illegal for a 16-year-old kid to make a porn film! In some states, like New York, it's still legal!

Urge churches, synagogues and service clubs to address the plight of homeless and exploited kids. Even more: ask your pastors, rabbis and community leaders to address thoughtfully the sexploitational attitudes encouraged and fostered by the media. What are your churches really doing for teenagers? Anything? See to it!

Sex isn't love and love isn't sex. It's good and beautiful when it's between married people who love each other and it's private. **Teach your kids about sex and family and marriage.** Do it early and often. Ask your churches to help if you aren't ready and willing. If you and your churches don't do it, don't object if our schools do!

Boycott your local video dealer if he rents hard-core porn. Almost all do.

If you're a parent worried about your kid and need help, call the Covenant House NINELINE, 1-800-999-9999. We'll do our best to help you.

A Gift To Be Embraced

Reflections on the
Covenant House Faith Community

The following was written by Alec Aspinwall, a former member of the Covenant House Faith Community in New York City.

Even after making the decision to visit the Covenant House Faith Community in New York City, I have to admit I was still somewhat suspicious. The closer I got to the address on Eighth Avenue in the heart of Times Square, in fact, the more my questions grew. What would draw normal people away from their comfortable lifestyles to pray for three hours a day and work with street kids while making $12 a week? What was drawing me?

For some time I had been searching for a way to deepen my relationship with God, and there was certainly something pushing me to take a closer look. Now, that courage seemed foolish and even a little frightening as I stood on the doorstep waiting for someone to answer the bell. I tried to look nonchalant, but as I glanced across the street, my eyes read the invitation posted on the door of the porno theater and I turned away in disgust — but without success. All around me, as I looked to the left and then to the right, the sorry sights and sounds of a string of "adult entertainment centers" made my stomach turn. I felt stunned. Is this where I had to live if I wanted to feel closer to God? Was I crazy? The eyes of the street people told me what I already knew. "You don't belong here," they said. They were right. I didn't belong here.

Then the door opened, and I was met with a warm smile. I tried to contain my gratitude for the timely rescue.

Once inside I was surprised by the size of the dwelling. It consisted of two six-story buildings joined by a large chapel. The dormitory-style living was neither elegant nor impoverished, but quite plain. The people I was soon to meet, however, were anything but plain.

I found myself in the midst of a Christian
"melting pot." There were nurses, teachers,
nuns, businesspeople, laborers, retired moth-
ers, and recent college graduates. They had
come from all over the country and even from
abroad. Although Catholic in prayer and wor-
ship, the Community also had members from
various Christian denominations. There were
conservatives and liberals, rich and not so rich,
young and the young at heart. Each had a different story to tell as to why they had come to
Covenant House, but their differences were
united by the call to strengthen their relationship with one God. To do so, they were willing
to accept the challenge of intense prayer (three
hours a day), communal living, and working
with the kids of Covenant House, whose lifestyle on the street can make them pretty tough
to deal with at times. They hurt so much that
sometimes the only way they can feel better
about themselves is to hurt you instead.

I had also expected Community members
to be a solemn bunch, bearing the weight of the
pervasive tragedy that surrounded them — but
I found just the opposite to be true. The Community had a vibrant spirit that was full of life
and laughter. Somehow the pain they were

daily exposed to had actually made room for
joy. I'm not saying that I didn't perceive their
own suffering, for many of them shared with
me the struggles they were experiencing with
the kids of Covenant House and with themselves. But they were beginning to see their
struggle no longer as a punishment to be en-
dured, but as a gift to be embraced. I began to
think that there might be something to that line
from the Gospel about how "dying to yourself
will bring new life."

By the end of the week, I had a lot to think
and pray about. Was I ready to commit to a
minimum of 13 months of three hours a day of
prayer? Could I dedicate myself to a simple
lifestyle in a chaste community? Was I able to
let go of the stability offered by my loved ones
and my career? Was I willing to be sent to any
one of the Covenant House sites assigned to me
and work at any job, whether it was working
directly with the kids or not? Most of all, could
I really love those hardened street kids and let
myself be touched by their pain?

I went home to California and asked God to
give me a sign. Something simple. An eclipse
maybe! No sign came. What did come, finally,
was a sense of peace that told me it was alright

to go against all the norms and ambitions ingrained in me and take a step forward in faith. After receiving a letter from the Orientation Director, I gave notice at my job and began to make plans to come back to New York.

It's hard to believe I've been here a year now. I've learned so much about myself, the kids, and God. I've learned, for instance, that drawing closer to God is a constant challenge and process. Street kids, I've come to learn, really have soft centers underneath those hard exteriors, and they often have more to teach me than I them. And God is always there, even though sometimes I don't recognize Him.

I still don't like the neighborhood, and I still get the same stares on the street that I did a year ago. Only now, sometimes I see Christ behind the cold eyes, and He reassures me, "You do belong here."

If you would like more information about joining the Faith Community, please write to Orientation Director of Faith Community, 346 West 17th Street, New York, NY 10011-5002, or call (212) 727-4000.

Need expert advice or support?

*Call our NINELINE counselors
at 1-800-999-9999.*

*We'll put you in touch with
people who can help you right
in your hometown.*

1-800-999-9999

This call is free.

*"I bound myself by oath, I made a covenant with you
. . . and you became mine."*　　　　*Ezekiel 16:8*

The only way to stop the pain and degradation of
street children is to get more people involved in
solutions to the devastating problems they face
every night of their lives.

　　After you read this book, please pass it along to
a friend. If you would like more copies, just fill out
this coupon and return it to us in the envelope provided. And know that because you took the time to
care, a kid won't have to sell himself to survive
tonight.

Please send me _____ **copies of** *Children of Eve*. **To help
defray the cost of sending you these books, we request a
minimum donation of $5 per book.**

Name _____

Address _____

City _____ **State** _____ **Zip** _____
*Please make your check payable to Covenant House.
Your gift is tax deductible.*

Many people like to charge their gift. If you would like to,
please fill out the information below:

I prefer to charge my: _____**MasterCard** _____**Visa**

Account # _____

Amount _____ **Exp. Date** _____

Signature _____

Mail to:　**Covenant House**
　　　　　　JAF Box 2973
　　　　　　New York, NY 10116-2973　　　FBKONZ

Or, call 1-800-388-3888 to charge your gift on your
MasterCard or Visa or to get more information.

> *"I bound myself by oath, I made a covenant with you ... and you became mine."*   **Ezekiel 16:8**

Covenant House depends almost entirely on gifts from friends like you to help 20,000 homeless and runaway children every year. We provide food, clothing, shelter, medical attention, educational and vocational training, and counseling to kids with no place to go for help. Please help if you can.

YES! I want to help the kids at Covenant House.
Here is my gift of: ☐ $10   ☐ $20   ☐ $25   ☐ Other

Name _____

Address _____

City _____ State _____ Zip _____

Please make your check payable to Covenant House.
Your gift is tax deductible.

Many people like to charge their gift. If you would like to, please fill out the information below:

I prefer to charge my: ____MasterCard ____Visa

Account # _____

Amount _____ **Exp. Date** _____

Signature _____

Mail to: **Covenant House**
          JAF Box 2973
          New York, NY 10116-2973   FBCVNZ

Or, call 1-800-388-3888 to charge your gift.

Copies of our financial and operating reports have been filed with the state and are available on request. To obtain one, simply write: NY Department of State, Charities Registration Section, 162 Washington Ave., Albany, NY 12231 or Covenant House, JAF Box 2973, New York, NY 10116-2973.

WV RESIDENTS: A copy of the official registration and supporting documents may be obtained from West Virginia Secretary of State, State Capitol, Charleston, WV 25305.

For II Set the tempting scene: voice confirms/cmt
doubt that Jesus was to Heaven Special Spokesman
& rep. (Heavy blow) ... to the 3? witness ... "others"
- If only such a certainty could be conveyed to each ... D.B.
Paul rec'd also a vision & ... that assured ... Must we
rely on their answer? pre-scientific information? Can the go

COVENANT HOUSE   give certainty also to ... ? Does how

346 West 17th Street   & doubt that, in effect, the question being

New York, NY 10011   raised by II Sets' audio readers?
                        Their doubts.

COVENANT HOUSE FLORIDA   How does he try to answer

733 Breakers Avenue   them? reassure them ...

Fort Lauderdale, FL 33304   (& ones)? By showing

                              1. That thru "J.C." the
COVENANT HOUSE NEW ORLEANS   "promises" of salvation
                              are guaranteed
611 North Rampart Street

New Orleans, LA 70112   [3] Da 53 "my
                              name is Strong

COVENANT HOUSE ALASKA   guaranteed to Rev to.
609 F Street ·   But in U 3 mere theory &
Anchorage, AK 99510   theology, is born out by
                          facts & life's experience!

COVENANT HOUSE CALIFORNIA He avoid answers that, but
1325 N. Western Avenue   can we go by that?

Hollywood, CA 90027   II Set is heavily infl. by an
                           excl — dif II Set 3 above —
COVENANT HOUSE TEXAS   an excl. more difficult now
1111 Lovett Boulevard   than then to find support for
Houston, TX 77006   the truth, "also they are to save"
                           The evil has not come — nor is
                           " new earth "

4   2. That doubt is relieved pretty
COVENANT HOUSE DONOR ASSISTANCE LINE: 1-800-388-3888
                           with practice etc then less. --
                           until can arrive then a place is their
                           losses, etc. \